Title VI

THE HINDENBURG

by
Tom Stacey

Illustrations by
Brian McGovern

LUCENT
B·O·O·K·S

WORLD DISASTERS

These and other titles are available in the Lucent World Disasters Series:

Library of Congress Cataloging-in-Publication Data

Stacey, Thomas, 1960-
    The Hindenburg / by Tom Stacey ; illustrations by Brian McGovern.
        p. cm. — (World disasters)
    Includes bibliographical references.
    Summary: Examines the aerial disaster of the Hindenburg zeppelin from a historical, scientific, and human perspective.
    ISBN 1-56006-010-7
    1. Hindenburg (Airship) 2. Aeronautics—Accidents—1937—Juvenile literature. [1. Hindenburg (Airship) 2. Airships.
3. Aeronautics—Accidents.] I. McGovern, Brian, ill. II. Title.
III. Series.
    TL659.H5S73 1990
    363.12'4—dc20   90-6256
                                                                          CIP
                                                                           AC

© Copyright 1990 by Lucent Books, Inc.
Lucent Books, Inc., P.O. Box 289011, San Diego, California, 92198-0011

For my brothers and sisters

Table of Contents

Preface
The World Disasters Series

World disasters have always aroused human curiosity. Whenever news of tragedy spreads, we want to learn more about it. We wonder how and why the disaster happened, how people reacted, and whether we might have acted differently. To be sure, disaster evokes a wide range of responses—fear, sorrow, despair, generosity, even hope. Yet from every great disaster, one remarkable truth always seems to emerge: in spite of death, pain, and destruction, the human spirit triumphs.

History is full of disasters, arising from a variety of causes. Earthquakes, floods, volcanic eruptions, and other natural events often produce widespread destruction. Just as often, however, people accidentally bring suffering and distress on themselves and other human beings. And many disasters have sinister causes, like human greed, envy, or prejudice.

The disasters included in this series have been chosen not only for their dramatic qualities, but also for their educational value. The reader will learn about the causes and effects of the greatest disasters in history. Technical concepts and interesting anecdotes are explained and illustrated in inset boxes.

But disasters should not be viewed in isolation. To enrich the reader's understanding, these books present historical information about the time period, and interesting facts about the culture in which each disaster occurred. Finally, they teach valuable lessons about human nature. More acts of bravery, cowardice, intelligence, and foolishness are compressed into the few days of a disaster than most people experience in a lifetime.

Dramatic illustrations and evocative narrative lure the reader to distant cities and times gone by. Readers witness the awesome power of an exploding volcano, the magnitude of a violent earthquake, and the hopelessness of passengers on a mighty ship passing to its watery grave. By reliving the events, the reader will see how disaster affects the lives of real people and will gain a deeper understanding of their sorrow, their pain, their courage, and their hope.

Introduction

Before May 6, 1937, the *Hindenburg* was the largest airship in the world and the creation of which Germany was proudest. A wonder to behold, it seemed stunning proof of the Germans' mastery of dirigible, or airship, technology. More than a technological triumph, however, the *Hindenburg* was also a powerful public relations tool. Germany saw the *Hindenburg,* which was the largest aircraft ever built, as a symbol of recovery from the humiliating conditions it was forced to accept after World War I. After years of hardship, the *Hindenburg* was something the Germans could be proud of. Simultaneously, a charismatic politician named Adolf Hitler was quickly gaining popularity by tapping into this same German pride.

During the mid-1930s, Hitler succeeded in capturing the support of the German people, despite his unjust policies of organized racism and violence. In 1937, Hitler's ambitions were on the rise for all the world to see. Similarly, the *Hindenburg* was becoming more visible and popular.

Wherever the *Hindenburg* went, people looked up and saw the zeppelin's giant tail fins decorated with

The Hindenburg Disaster in History

1783
First hydrogen-filled balloon flight

1784
Frenchman Jean Meusnier flies first propeller-driven balloon

1852
French inventor Henri Giffard builds the first power-driven airship

1871
Otto van Bismarck becomes first chancellor of Germany

1872
German Paul Haenlein flies first gasoline-powered dirigible

1884
Frenchmen Charles Renard and Arthur Krebs build and fly the first battery-powered airship, *La France*

1900
German Count Ferdinand von Zeppelin builds the first rigid-style airship

1903
Wright brothers successfully fly first heavier-than-air plane at Kitty Hawk

1914
World War I begins

1915
Germans use airships to bomb England

1919
First transatlantic crossing by an airship, the English-built *R-34*

1921
U.S. Navy flies first helium-filled blimp

the swastika, the emblem of Hitler's Nazi party. The swastika was not yet known the world over as a symbol of hatred and cruelty; in time, however, it would be burned into the memory of humankind.

On May 6, 1937, at the end of its first transatlantic trip of the season, the *Hindenburg* exploded and burned while docking at Lakehurst, New Jersey. In just thirty-four seconds, the inferno destroyed the once-mighty *Hindenburg* and thirty-six people died. Its fiery end on that spring day remains one of the most famous disasters ever.

The incident was officially classified as an accident. Unofficially, many suspected sabotage. What really caused the *Hindenburg* disaster? Was it the result of a fatal flaw in the design of hydrogen-filled dirigibles? Could it have been a freak accident? Or was it the act of someone striking out against Hitler, long before the rest of the world recognized his evil?

Like accounts of other disasters, such as that of the *Titanic* or the *Challenger* space shuttle, the story of the *Hindenburg* is one of great faith in technology and perhaps also of excessive pride that leads to horrible tragedy. It is a story that must be told, for the tragedy also holds lessons for all of humanity.

1923
Shenandoah, the first U.S.-made rigid airship, built

1925
Gėrman war hero Paul von Hindenburg becomes president of Germany

1929
German airship *Graf Zeppelin* travels twenty-thousand miles around the world

1933
German President von Hindenburg names Adolf Hitler chancellor of Germany

1937
The *Hindenburg* explodes while landing in Lakehurst, N.J.; 36 die

1939
World War II begins

1949
West Germany and East Germany become separate states

1961
U.S. armed services airship program terminated; Berlin Wall built

1965
Goodyear builds blimp *Mayflower* for advertising

1973
East and West Germany join United Nations

1989
Berlin Wall torn down

1990
East and West Germany take steps toward reunification

One
A Fabulous Invention

Imagine a balloon as wide as a large house and about three city blocks long. Picture it floating through the sky overhead, at times blotting out the sun, and you begin to appreciate the immensity of the *Hindenburg*. It was the largest dirigible ever built. While its gigantic cigar-shaped size was its distinctive characteristic, the *Hindenburg* also had many other features that made it the premier dirigible of all time.

Like other German-built dirigibles, the *Hindenburg* was kept afloat by large bags filled with hydrogen gas. The bags hung from an intricate skeletonlike frame of lightweight metal. Because of its huge size—803 feet long and 135 feet in diameter—the *Hindenburg* was able to carry more hydrogen gas than other dirigibles. As a re-

sult, it was able to carry a large load of passengers and supplies.

A silver-coated gray fabric cover stretched over the *Hindenburg*'s entire frame. Thrust, or forward movement, was provided by four lightweight but powerful and efficient diesel engines. Each engine churned a twenty-foot wooden propeller through the air, enabling the *Hindenburg* to cruise at eighty-four miles an hour. It could travel eleven thousand miles without refueling—much farther than airplanes of its day. This was because the *Hindenburg* did not need to use fuel to keep itself afloat; the hydrogen gas did that. Therefore, all the fuel it carried could be used for propulsion. These qualities made the *Hindenburg* well-suited to carry passengers.

Soon after it was built in 1933, the *Hindenburg* gained a reputation as the best way to travel. A two-deck hull built into the *Hindenburg*'s frame contained twenty-five passenger cabins, a dining room, lounge, bar, smoking room, shower rooms, kitchen, and accommodations for the crew. Passengers enjoyed the gourmet meals and leisurely sight-seeing that was available on the dirigible.

A Floating Five Star Hotel

Traveling on the *Hindenburg* was a luxurious experience. It was like staying in a floating five-star hotel. The *Hindenburg* provided regular round-trip passenger service to South America and to the United States from Germany. Because of

In Berlin, the *Hindenburg* (left) and the *Graf Zeppelin* take part in a Nazi
propaganda demonstration in 1936.

its popularity, the *Hindenburg* became a common sight to people on the ground. When they saw this shimmering giant balloon floating through the sky, they marveled at the ingenuity that created the *Hindenburg*. Who could have dreamed of such a thing? Who built it, and why?

The technology that allowed the *Hindenburg* to fly was developed in 1900 by Count Ferdinand von Zeppelin. Because of his interest in new technology, Zeppelin was known as the 'crazy old count'. Zeppelin first became interested in lighter-than-air flight as a result of a chance encounter with a balloonist in the United States in 1863.

An officer in the German cavalry, Zeppelin came to the United States with apparently no interest in flight whatsoever. A professional soldier, he traveled across the ocean because he saw an opportunity to gain valuable fighting experience in the United States Civil War. He joined forces with the Union Army and did fight for a brief time. But he soon grew bored with the war and decided to explore the American wilderness instead.

Zeppelin organized a small expedition to seek out the source of the Mississippi River. During this trip he stopped at a hotel in Minneapolis, Minnesota. Looking out

Ferdinand von Zeppelin (in felt hat) traveled to the United States to fight with the Union Army during the Civil War.

of his hotel window one day, he saw a large, hydrogen-filled balloon floating in the air. He rushed to the window, immediately fascinated by the balloon and the possibility of flight.

Could Be Useful in War

The next day, Zeppelin arranged for a ride in the balloon. It was a wonderful feeling to float high above the treetops and to be able to see everything for miles around. Zeppelin began to wonder if such a balloon could be useful in war. He reasoned that from high up in the sky, a soldier could keep track of enemy troop movements and drop bombs on the targeted sites.

In 1898, thirty-five years after he was first struck with the idea, Zeppelin designed his first dirigible. Constructed of a lightweight aluminum frame that would hold bags filled with lighter-than-air hydrogen gas, it combined the lift of a balloon, the thrust of a propeller, and the steering qualities of a rudder. The addition of the rudder gave the pilot more control than was possible with a balloon, which was entirely dependent upon the wind. Zeppelin's design became the model for all dirigibles to follow, including the *Hindenburg*.

Zeppelin formed a corporation and used his personal fortune to finance the construction of his dirigible, called *Luftschiffe Zeppelin I*, the *Airship Zeppelin*, or *LZ 1*. It was first flown at the village of Manzell, near the town of Friedrichshafen. Zeppelin had invited some

Count Ferdinand von Zeppelin, the inventor of the first steerable dirigible.

military officials to observe the *LZ 1*'s first flight. He was hoping to sell his invention to the German government.

Zeppelin managed to keep *LZ 1* afloat for eighteen minutes but had a difficult time keeping the airship level. Finally, after nose-diving several times, he was forced to land. Like most who saw the test flight over Lake Constance on the first weekend of July 1900, the military officials were very disappointed. A newspaper reporter from Frankfurt wrote that the flight was "extremely interesting" but "proved conclusively that a dirigible balloon is of practically no value."

This conclusion was exactly the opposite of the impression that

EVOLUTION OF LIGHTER-THAN-AIR SHIPS—1783-1900

The dirigible started out as non-rigid, or as a huge hydrogen-filled balloon with no internal structure. It then advanced to a semirigid structure, and had a lightweight metal keel along the bottom. This keel allowed for the construction of larger, more stable dirigibles. Finally, Zeppelin came up with a rigid design with a complete metal skeleton and a sturdier keel. Since the metal skeleton maintained the ship's shape, the gas could be stored in small cells rather than in large balloons.

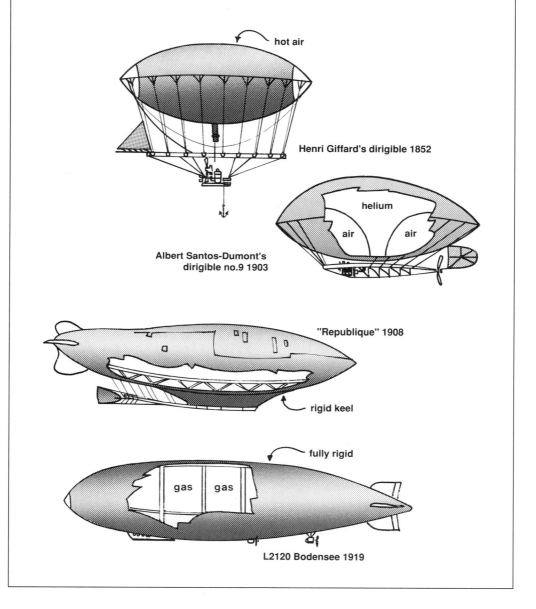

hot air

Henri Giffard's dirigible 1852

helium

air   air

Albert Santos-Dumont's dirigible no.9 1903

"Republique" 1908

rigid keel

fully rigid

gas   gas

L2120 Bodensee 1919

Zeppelin wanted to give. But he did not abandon his plan. He brought the *LZ 1* out for two more flights. He managed to keep the dirigible in the air for one hour and a half on the second flight, reaching a speed of seventeen miles per hour. Still, this performance was not enough to convince government officials of the dirigible's value. They were not interested.

Mixed Results

Several more successes and failures followed. In January 1906, Zeppelin succeeded in flying his next dirigible, the *LZ 2*. Unfortunately, the *LZ 2* came to a disastrous end when both of its engines failed on its first flight out, forcing it to land. High winds on the ground quickly destroyed it. Zeppelin followed this failure with the relative success of the *LZ 3*.

The *LZ 3* was identical to the *LZ 2*, except that two horizontal fins had been added in the stern of the ship. With this addition, the *LZ 3* was able to stay in flight for eight hours, breaking all previous duration records. The dirigible was able to cruise at twenty-four miles per hour and could carry eleven people. Unfortunately, the *LZ 4*, Zeppelin's next dirigible, was not as successful. In 1908, on its first flight, the *LZ 4* was forced to land because of high winds. While on the ground, it brushed against a tree, tearing open one of its gas cells. It burst into flames and was quickly destroyed. Miraculously, this disaster had the effect of encouraging public support for Zeppelin and his inventions. In fact, Zeppelin later referred to the incident as his "luckiest unlucky day."

A tremendous outpouring by the

Zeppelin's new airship during its successful trial trip over Lake Constance.

The *LZ 129* outside its hangar in Friedrichshafen, Germany in 1936. The *LZ 129* was built to carry passengers from Germany to Lakehurst, New Jersey.

HOW DOES A DIRIGIBLE FLY?

Count Zeppelin's dirigibles were made in a fish-like shape, so that air would flow smoothly over the hull. Zeppelins, like airplanes, used movable flaps, called elevators, that were attached to horizontal tail fins. When the elevators were turned up, air pushing against them made the tail of the zeppelin dip, and the nose rise. With the elevators turned down, the tail rose, and the nose dipped. Other movable flaps, called rudders, were attached to the vertical tail fins. They were used to steer the airship to the left and the right, just like the rudder on a boat.

Zeppelins could also be made to rise or sink by controlling the amount of weight they carried. Before a zeppelin took off, large bags of water called ballast were stored in front and rear. When the captain wanted the ship to rise quickly, he could release ballast. He could also release small amounts of ballast from one tank or the other in order to balance the ship. The captain could also release hydrogen out of valves on top of the hydrogen bags to lower the ship. At high altitudes the pressure on the bags would decrease, and the gas inside would expand. In this case the valves would automatically open and release hydrogen. The captain would then have to release ballast, or the ship would sink as soon as the pressure was increased.

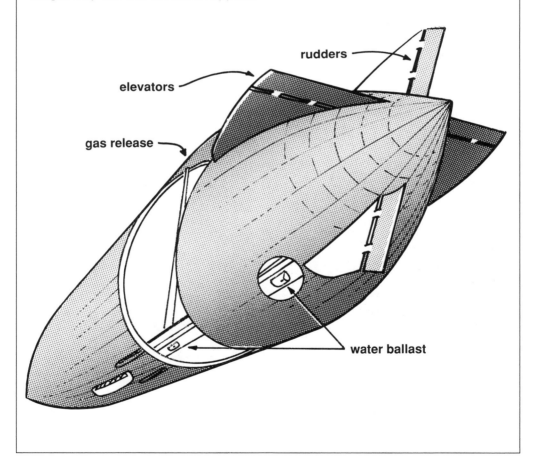

elevators

rudders

gas release

water ballast

German people followed the *LZ 4* accident. Civic leaders, workers, schoolchildren, and politicians contributed money to Zeppelin's cause. The Zeppelin Corporation was in much better financial shape than ever before. The German people wanted Zeppelin to succeed.

Zeppelin did not receive the same kind of popular support from the military, however, and it was for military purposes that Zeppelin had built his dirigibles. His advisers encouraged him to change his mind and use his airships for passenger flight. Zeppelin finally agreed, and in 1909 the first airline, the German Airship Transport Company (or DELAG) was born.

HYDROGEN FILLED THE FIRST DIRIGIBLES

Hydrogen is the colorless, odorless, tasteless and highly explosive gas discovered by Henry Cavendish in 1766. The most abundant element in the universe, hydrogen occurs on earth chiefly in combination with oxygen, in water. Hydrogen can be produced by passing steam over heated carbon, such as coal. It is composed of only two particles, the smallest number that can form a neutral atom. Its nucleus consists of a single proton bearing a positive electrical charge.

DELAG provided travel service between Germany's major cities. The flights were leisurely affairs, complete with champagne and

The *LZ 1* takes off with a full load of passengers.

caviar. With these new flights, the dirigible's popularity increased. People sang and cheered whenever they saw one of the dirigibles flying overhead. Germans dubbed the dirigibles "zeppelins" and bought cigarettes, coats, caps, and other items imprinted with the now famous ship.

Zeppelin advanced the development of dirigibles by transforming an uncontrollable balloon into a permanent hull of vast size and lifting power that could be propelled by an engine and steered by a rudder. Because of Zeppelin's work, Germany led the world in dirigible development from the introduction of the *LZ 1* in 1900 to the last flight of the *Hindenburg* in 1937.

Two

The Rise of Hitler

During World War I, Germany was successful in using its zeppelins in war, just as Zeppelin himself had envisioned. But the fast-paced development of airplanes quickly made the dirigibles obsolete. An airplane could easily drop explosives on the huge dirigibles, which would ignite the hydrogen gas that filled them. The zeppelins would be destroyed in seconds.

The ability to fight wars from the air, however, dramatically changed battle techniques. Before, battles were fought by professional soldiers, far from civilians. In World War I, airplanes and dirigibles attacked cities, killing civilians by the thousands and inflicting unprecedented damage on these urban populations. When the war was finally finished in 1918, no one had really won. There were only losers. Germany had helped to start the war, terrorizing the skies with its zeppelins. The Allies decided that Germany should be the biggest loser and the country was severely punished for its involvement.

The fighting nations concluded the war with the Treaty of Versailles. The treaty forced Germany to admit that it had started the war. It imposed many conditions on Germany, including specific rules forbidding it to make any more dirigibles. France and Britain seized any remaining zeppelins that had survived the war. (Unfortunately, pilots in these countries did not know how to operate the delicate zeppelins properly and quickly destroyed them in careless accidents.)

There were also other severe postwar restrictions on Germany. For the next fifteen years, the French were granted the right to occupy the German region along the Rhine River. Germany had to turn over other pieces of land to several of its neighbors. Additionally, Germany was forced to pay large reparations, money to compensate for damages, to other countries involved in the war. Suffering from heavy war damage, these additional financial burdens caused Germany's economy to collapse.

German money, or marks, became so worthless that even a railroad car full of currency would not buy a loaf of bread. A thousand billion marks equaled one prewar mark. Throughout Germany, hunger, unemployment, and antigovernment sentiment grew. Various political parties struggled for power, and extremist

Adolf Hitler, during a World War II motorcade, waves to the crowds who have come to see him. Hitler was tremendously popular with the German people.

groups such as the Communists and the Nazis became popular.

As the German economy crumbled, so did the self-esteem of the German people. Germans felt ashamed and humiliated by the provisions in the Treaty of Versailles. They began to feel that the ruinous state of their country had been unjustly forced upon them. The Germans' bitterness and disenchantment increased throughout the 1920s, as a worldwide economic depression took hold. Late in that decade, a politician emerged who excited the German people with his fiery speeches. His name was Adolf Hitler.

A Superior Race

Hitler denounced the Treaty of Versailles and claimed that the Germans were a superior race. He promised to create a new Germany that the people could be proud of again. This was a welcome message to the Germans who felt cheated by the treaty. They felt that their country had been punished enough by the war and should not be forced to continue paying reparations or be occupied by foreign countries. Hitler recognized these dissatisfactions, and the popularity of his Nazi party increased.

In 1933, the president of Germany, Paul von Hindenburg, died shortly after he appointed Hitler chancellor. This allowed Hitler an opportunity to try to gain more power. Through his sheer charisma as a speaker, Hitler was able to harness the Germans' sense of national

Adolf Hitler built his popularity on the German people's dissatisfaction with the terms of the Treaty of Versailles.

pride. Riding a wave of popular support, he managed to abolish the presidency and create a dictatorship. He called himself the fuhrer, or leader.

Under Hitler's rule, prosperity began to return to Germany. Hitler put many people to work in his attempt to rebuild Germany's military forces. He hired people to rebuild the German airplanes, weapons, and tanks, and all of this activity gave a boost to the economy. He employed all of Germany's young men by requiring them to undergo military training, rebuilding the army and air force in the process. While these changes benefited the German people, they were strictly in violation of the Treaty of Versailles, which limited the number of troops and weapons Germany could accumulate. Hitler made no secret of his contempt for the treaty and openly violated it.

Propaganda a Key Weapon

With the installation of a dictatorship, Hitler began to censor any ideas that did not correspond to his own. In order to enforce this censorship, he created the position of minister of propaganda and named Joseph Goebbels to the post. Propaganda became a key weapon of the Nazi party, and Goebbels was its master. He carefully orchestrated rallies where Hitler gave speeches about a reborn Germany that would rise from the ashes of 1918. These speeches enthralled listeners, creating a fury of nationalism.

Goebbels also produced films

Joseph Goebbels, the minister of propaganda under Hitler's regime.

21

U.S. DIRIGIBLE TECHNOLOGY

The Americans combined two flight technologies in their experiments with dirigibles as aircraft carriers. Airplanes were launched from a bay in the belly of a dirigible. They would fly off and zoom over the enemy, then return to the airship to refuel. To board the dirigible, the airplane pilot would fly slowly under it, carefully attach the plane to a hook, then turn off the engines. The hook was attached to a crane, which pulled the plane into the belly of the ship, where there was a hangar. It was a good idea that never caught on.

A private U.S. company also became involved in dirigible technology when the Luftschiffbau entered into a contract with the Goodyear Tire and Rubber Company, creating the Goodyear Zeppelin Company. Goodyear made use of the Zeppelin Company's patents. An important difference was that American dirigibles were designed to contain helium, a lighter-than-air gas that is not flammable, like oxygen. This would make American dirigibles safer than the hydrogen-filled German models.

This rare U.S. Air Force photo shows a Navy airship with a plane launching from below.

that depicted Germans as blue-eyed, blond-haired, superior people, dedicated to the greater glory of Germany. He controlled the theater and the press and forbade anything to be said or printed that was not acceptable to the Nazi party. Gradually, the propaganda achieved Goebbels's aims. Many Germans became swept up in the excitement that Hitler and the Nazis created. Deprived of objective sources of news and culture, individuals began to believe they were a master race capable of anything.

In his constant search for new

The giant *Hindenburg* sails serenely over New York City in 1937.

DIRIGIBLES DURING WORLD WAR I

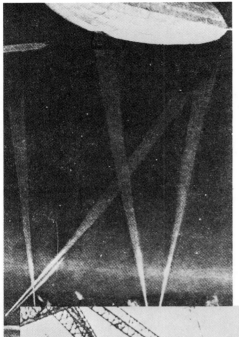

Germany's dirigibles were successfully used for a brief time during World War I. Left, a zeppelin performs a bombing raid over London, England. Below, a wrecked zeppelin after being shot down over England. The rapid development of the airplane during World War I made the use of dirigibles obsolete. The dirigible simply could not compete with the faster, more maneuverable airplane.

ways to project the Nazi party's image, Goebbels turned to the zeppelins as a possibility. Since zeppelins were uniquely German and a symbol of the better times before World War I, he believed they would make effective propaganda tools. The postwar restrictions on building zeppelins had been lifted, and the newest ones were even bigger and better than their prewar counterparts. Since Zeppelin's death in 1917, the Zeppelin Corporation had been run by Hugo Eckener, a former sailor. Eckener had continued to make advances with the zeppelin, developing the *Graf Zeppelin,* which he piloted on a journey around the world. Because of his success, Eckener was somewhat of a worldwide celebrity. At the time that Goebbels was looking for a new propaganda symbol, Eckener was developing a newer, more powerful zeppelin that would utilize the latest technology.

A Powerful Nation

Goebbels thought this new zeppelin could be used to show the superiority of German technology. He believed that it would persuade Germans and others that Germany was emerging as a powerful nation.

Goebbels contributed $500,000 in government funds toward the completion of the new zeppelin. As far as he was concerned, the new zeppelin's only function would be to help increase the popularity of Hitler's regime. To further this end, Goebbels ordered that swastikas be placed on the 150-foot tail surfaces

Dr. Hugo Eckener was well-known as a master builder and navigator of the zeppelin. Eckener would be on board the *Hindenburg's* last flight.

of the zeppelin. The swastika was the symbol of the Nazi party, which became bolder and more oppressive as Hitler tightened his grip on the German people.

To Eckener, it was an outrage to have swastikas painted on the new airship, which he named the *Hindenburg*. He was absolutely against the idea of using the *Hindenburg* as a propaganda tool. The opposition of Eckener and Goebbels resulted in a confrontation. It happened shortly after Eckener had completed work on the *Hindenburg*. Goebbels decided to mobilize both the *Hindenburg* and the *Graf Zep-pelin* in a propaganda effort. He wanted both zeppelins to fly over every city in Germany, dropping leaflets that praised Hitler and blaring patriotic music over loudspeakers. Goebbels believed the stunt would arouse the nationalistic fervor of the German people.

On the day that the propaganda flight was to begin, there was a strong wind blowing. Under pressure from Goebbels, Capt. Ernest Lehmann decided to take the *Hindenburg* out, despite the danger presented by the winds. As it was being taken out of the hangar, the tail section of the zeppelin was blown side-

Goebbels insisted on having swastikas painted on the tail fins of the *Hindenburg* as a propaganda stunt. Eckener, president of the Zeppelin Corporation, strongly objected.

ways into the building. The damage was quickly repaired and the flight went on. But when Eckener found out about the incident, he was furious. In front of the *Hindenburg*'s crew and members of Hitler's secret police, called SS, Eckener sternly reprimanded Lehmann for his lack of caution. Eckener made it clear that he was especially upset that the *Hindenburg* would be put at risk for something as stupid as a propaganda flight. The SS men reported his tirade back to Goebbels, who demanded to see Eckener.

Goebbels told Eckener that the Third Reich would not tolerate any dissent. He threatened Eckener, saying that he would have been severely punished if he had not been so popular with the German people. Goebbels then declared that Eckener's name would never again be mentioned by German newspapers or on radio. Goebbels had effectively made Eckener a nonperson.

Goebbels's reprimand was meant to show Eckener that it was the Nazi party, and not Eckener, that ran the Zeppelin Corporation. Goebbels made it clear that whenever he needed the zeppelins, he would use them.

Three

An Uneventful Flight

It was to be a typical flight for the *Hindenburg* that waited on the loading dock on May 3, 1937. Passengers and crew members stood in the shadow of the giant airship as they prepared to board the *Hindenburg* for its first voyage of the year to the United States.

One by one, the thirty-six passengers followed each other up a stairway leading into the belly of the vast, plump, silvery ship. At the top of the stairs, they entered the hull, a double-decked structure attached to the bottom of the ship. At about 7:30 P.M., when the last person climbed on board, the hinged staircase was folded in half and pulled up inside the hull. Capt. Max Pruss stuck his head out of the open window of the control car at the bottom of the hull and put a mega-

phone to his mouth. "Up ship!" he shouted. The men of the ground crew released the cables that were holding the zeppelin on the ground. Passengers at the windows in the hull called and waved to people on the ground as the zeppelin began floating quietly up into the sky. The crew efficiently reeled in the cables and stored them away.

When the *Hindenburg* reached about three hundred feet, Captain Pruss gave the order to start the engines. In four cars suspended from different parts of the underside of the airship, big diesel engines coughed and sputtered. Each of the engines turned over and began humming smoothly. The twenty-one foot propeller at the back of each engine car began slicing through the air. The massive airship moved forward through the darkening sky.

The *Hindenburg* was again on its way. The premier airship in the world began its climb to a cruising altitude of about seven hundred feet as Captain Pruss set a course for the Rhine River. Dusk settled as the airship sailed over the German countryside.

Fastest Way to Travel

Inside, passengers made themselves comfortable in the lightweight aluminum and canvas chairs in the ship's lounge. They marveled at the smooth ride. In 1937, it was the fastest, most reliable, most comfortable way to travel. Some of the passengers were on business, like Edward Douglas, an American advertising executive working on a big

The huge *Hindenburg* is completed on March 7, 1936. It could accommodate 200 day passengers or 50 overnight.

Capt. Ernest Lehmann on board the *Hindenburg.*

account for General Motors. Others were vacationing, like Mr. and Mrs. Otto Ernst. They planned to spend a week in New York, then fly back to Germany. Margaret Mather, an older unmarried woman who loved to travel, was also vacationing. Joseph Spah, a professional acrobat and comedian, was returning to his family in the United States after having performed in Europe.

Other passengers were mixing business and pleasure. Through an arrangement with the Zeppelin Corporation, professional photographer Karl Otto Clemens was trading his services for a reduced fare. Also on board were journalists Leonhard and Gertrude Adelt. Leonhard Adelt's opinions had gotten him in trouble with the Nazi government. But now he was working as the aviation editor of the German publica-

tion *Deutsche Allegemeine.* He hoped to stay out of trouble by covering technical developments that were not controversial. He was also collaborating with his friend Capt. Ernest Lehmann on Lehmann's autobiography.

A senior official of the Zeppelin Corporation, Lehmann happened to be on board too. For Lehmann, this ride should have been just like any of the many others he had taken. But it was not. On that day, he carried in his pocket a copy of a letter from Kathie Rauch, a tavern owner in Milwaukee, Wisconsin. Originally addressed to the German embassy in Washington, D.C., a copy of the letter had been sent to Lehmann. The letter said that the *Hindenburg* "will be destroyed by a time bomb during a flight to another country. Please believe my words as the truth, so that later no one will have cause for regret."

Other Threats to Zeppelins

Lehmann was concerned. There had been other threats to Germany's zeppelins. But this one seemed more real. Especially since only a year before, a bomb had been found in the dining room of the *Graf Zeppelin* as it sat on the ground in Rio de Janeiro. Fortunately, that bomb was dismantled before it had a chance to explode.

Because of this threat the *Hindenburg* had been carefully inspected a few hours before takeoff by Hitler's secret police. Crew members, unaware of the threat, thought the search was pointless. To the crew, the SS men seemed unprepared. Whatever they were searching for, they certainly would not know where to look for it among the miles of cable, wire, metal tubing, and fabric bags that made up the *Hindenburg.* The giant airship was an intricate maze. It would only confound anyone who did not know it intimately—as the crew members did. The crew was not surprised when the SS men found nothing.

When their search did not turn up a bomb, officials of the SS met with Lehmann and other officials of the Zeppelin Corporation on the morning of May 3. They considered canceling the flight, but the SS was against the idea. To cancel the first

Passengers disembark and the mail is unloaded from the *Graf Zeppelin*. The ship's officers can be seen inside the gondola.

flight of the season would attract too much negative attention. Germany would not accept the embarrassment of postponing the flight. They would go ahead, and do their best to stop any attempts to destroy the *Hindenburg*. As a precaution, Captain Lehmann had been thoroughly briefed on the situation by SS officers.

During their investigation into the mysterious letter, the SS men had prepared background checks on several passengers whom they considered suspicious. They told Lehmann that he should watch several passengers closely during the flight. Also, until departure time, an armed guard was stationed outside the hangar to keep an eye on the *Hindenburg*. With these orders, Lehmann worriedly gave the order for preparations for the flight to continue.

A Few Small Sacrifices

Flying on a hydrogen-filled airship required a few small sacrifices of its passengers. For instance, security guards confiscated any matches or cigarette lighters. An inferno could result if even the smallest flame came in contact with the extremely flammable hydrogen gas that kept the ship afloat. The guards also took flashbulbs, which could possibly trigger a spark. They even confiscated flashlight batteries. They took away objects like the steel tip of a cane, which could get caught and rip the fabric of the ship or even cause a dangerous spark by coming in contact with another piece of metal.

On this trip, soldiers insisted on thoroughly examining and X-raying every single piece of luggage.

After they passed their customs and safety inspections, passengers came on board to the B deck. A bronze bust of Field Marshall Paul von Hindenburg, the late president for whom the zeppelin was named, greeted passengers as they stepped on board. On the right, a windowed aisle led to the shower rooms and to the bar entrance. Through the bar was the smoking room. Although it might seem a dangerous luxury on a zeppelin full of highly combustible hydrogen, the *Hindenburg's* smoking room was perfectly safe.

An air-locked chamber between the bar and smoking room effectively sealed the room off from the rest of the ship and prevented the leakage of any hydrogen into the room. There was one cigarette lighter, the heated coil type found in cars, chained to the counter. For pipe smokers, the bartender kept matches, which he held onto very tightly. He also examined each person as he or she left to make sure that no burning materials left the smoking room.

The walls of the smoking room were decorated with pictures of famous airships, including the pioneer ships of the Montgolfier brothers, Jacques Charles, and Alberto Santos-Dumont. There were also pictures of the *LZ 1* and other famous German zeppelins. Surrounded by these images of the glorious past, passengers must have felt

These photographs were taken on board the *Hindenburg* in 1936. Above is the dining saloon during lunchtime. Below, two passengers are absorbed in a game of chess.

On board the *Hindenburg*, passengers work in the writing room.

that they were part of a piece of floating history.

Clear plastic windows were placed in the floor of the B deck. Passengers could look straight down to the earth below. Some passengers were understandably wary of these windows in the floor. By instinct, they did not want to get too close, for fear that they might fall through. To ease these anxieties, crew members would jump up and down on the windows to prove they were safe.

Upstairs, the A deck contained the passenger cabins, the library, the dining room, and the lounge. Some of the *Hindenburg*'s passen-

gers milled about in the lounge as the trip began. The outside wall of the lounge was lined with large windows that slanted out and up. On the wall opposite the windows, a big map allowed passengers to chart the progress of their journey. It was a comfortable room, and people gathered by the windows to watch as lights twinkled on in village homes below. As they floated upward, the passengers were amazed that they felt no sensation of movement.

Besides the *Hindenburg*'s thirty-six paying passengers, there were sixty-one crew members aboard. These included seven stewards, four cooks, seventeen mechanics, and three engineering officers. There were also additional flight officers on board. They were being trained so that they would be ready to operate the two new airships being built by the Zeppelin Corporation. Corporate officials anticipated a growing demand for transatlantic flight, and they wanted to be ready.

After a short while, the lights of a city appeared below. Observant passengers noticed by the still picture beneath them that the ship's progress had come to a halt. The airship had stopped to drop a bag of mail over the city of Cologne, on the Rhine in western Germany. Each letter in the sack was postmarked by the *Hindenburg*'s on-board post office, then bundled into a sack that was parachuted overboard. The ship's searchlight followed the mailbag as it drifted down to the ground. Then the engines came back to life, and the *Hindenburg* continued on its way.

Finally, the *Hindenburg* reached the North Atlantic. The great ship cruised at a speed of ninety miles an hour, with virtually no vibration. At 10 P.M. the stewards served a light snack of cold meats, salad, and wine. Afterward, most of the passengers retired to their rooms and went to bed in the staterooms on the A deck. Much like the rooms on Pullman railroad cars, each of the twenty-five staterooms had upper

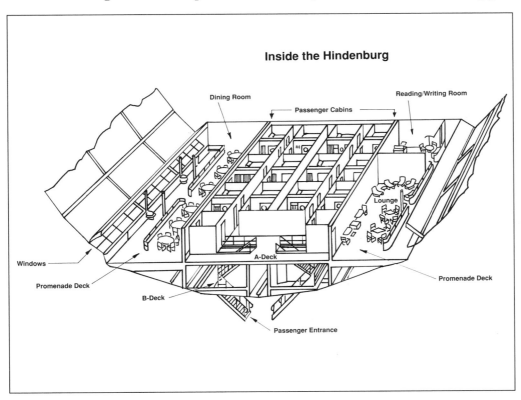

Inside the Hindenburg

Dining Room

Reading/Writing Room

Passenger Cabins

Lounge

Windows

Promenade Deck

A-Deck

Promenade Deck

B-Deck

Passenger Entrance

and lower bunks and a sink with hot and cold running water. The upper bunk could be folded into the wall during the day. The lower bunk could also be used as a table for writing and playing cards.

During the *Hindenburg*'s first night out of Frankfurt, three passengers stayed up late and sat in the bar. In the command car, members of the ship's crew took turns standing watch, four hours on and four hours off. A storm front had been spotted over the ocean, and the crew looked for a hole in the clouds where the airship could go through. They could not find one. Captain Pruss thought about skirting around the storm, but decided to simply go through it.

A Little Experiment

Some passengers heard the soft sound of rain falling on the ship's linen covering as they lay in bed. But still the ship's ride was exceptionally smooth and level. In fact, during a previous transatlantic flight some one had performed a little experiment that showed just how smooth the ride was: when the *Hindenburg* left Germany, a milk bottle was set upside down on a table to see how long it would stay upright. The bottle was still standing when the airship landed at its destination, Lakehurst, New Jersey.

In the morning, passengers enjoyed freshly baked rolls, eggs, sausage, cheeses, fruits, and coffee in the *Hindenburg*'s elegant dining room, situated upstairs on A deck. The dining room was fifteen by fifty

feet and sat thirty-four people. Meals were served there in two shifts. Passengers may have felt like they were in a small, intimate restaurant. The tables were laid with white linen napkins and tablecloths. On each table stood a bouquet of fresh-cut flowers. Fine silverware accompanied the special china dinnerware. The service and the food were first-rate.

Luxury Did Not Come Cheap

This kind of luxury did not come cheap, however. Tickets for the flight were $400 one way and $720 round-trip. The prices were $680 and $1,224 for a private room. The fare included the *Hindenburg*'s gourmet cuisine. A typical lunch menu consisted of strong broth, Bavarian-style roast duckling, cabbage, savory potatoes and gravy, pears, and mocha. Dinner might start with a cream soup and then include grilled sole with parsley butter; venison cutlets with potatoes, mushrooms, and cream sauce; and a mixed cheese plate served with a selection of German and French wines and champagnes.

The *Hindenburg* carried about 5,550 pounds of food, including fresh meat and poultry, fish, sausage, cold cuts, potatoes, fresh vegetables, eggs, butter, cheese, marmalade, canned goods, and milk. The kitchen was well-equipped with electric roasting and baking ovens, where bread was baked fresh daily.

Other small services were included in the *Hindenburg*'s exorbitant fare. Each night, stewards picked up passengers' shoes left outside each cabin and returned them polished in the morning. In each cabin there was a button that would summon a steward, who would bring wine or playing cards, and do anything else to make a passenger relaxed and contented.

Captain Pruss had a saying that summed up the atmosphere on board the zeppelin: "If you want to travel quickly, take an airplane. If you want to travel comfortably, take an airship."

It also seemed a safe way to travel. The *Graf Zeppelin* alone had logged more than one million miles without any passenger fatalities. Furthermore, the *Hindenburg* had es-tablished its own record of safety and comfort with eleven uneventful flights between Germany and the United States in 1936. The experienced Captain Pruss had been at the helm of sixteen transatlantic voyages, including several across the South Atlantic to Rio de Janeiro. He was noted for his skill and precision in landing the giant aircraft. Pruss had learned the art of piloting from Eckener, the head of the Zeppelin Corporation.

Certain that traveling by airship was safe, many passengers relaxed in the lounge, where it was fascinating to look out of the windows. A constant panorama of sights was always unfolding below. They could

Through the windows, passengers could hear dogs barking at them 500 feet below the giant ship.

hear dogs bark and car horns honk at the ship. Wherever they went—over cities, pastures, mountains, or forests—the passengers would see people looking up at them, waving. On one trip they saw someone riding a bicycle who kept looking up at the ship while pedaling along. Finally, the fascinated bicyclist crashed into a roadside hedge.

A Great Silver Whale

On this trip out over the Atlantic, however, there was not much to look at. The *Hindenburg*'s passengers watched the waves below as the reflection of the airship tagged along like a great silver whale. The weather was drizzly and gray for the most part, and the *Hindenburg* was forced to fight a strong head wind all the way across the Atlantic. With no real scenery to view, passengers occupied themselves by playing cards and sitting in the lounge.

Chief radio operator Willie Speck and his crew monitored the airwaves for weather information and radioed the *Hindenburg*'s position to Hamburg every fifteen minutes. They also handled private messages for passengers who sent and received telegrams to and from relatives and business contacts. Taking an incoming message for Edward Douglas, the advertising executive, Speck noticed that it was in some sort of code. He alerted Captain Lehmann.

Lehmann remembered that the SS men suspected that Douglas was not really an advertising executive. They thought he was a spy, sent to

Germany to collect information on German industry. Alerted to the strange telegrams Douglas was now receiving, Lehmann made a note to watch him closely.

Another suspect who was acting suspiciously was passenger Joseph Spah. Spah insisted on visiting his dog, which was stored away in a room inside the ship. The first time he visited his dog, he was escorted to the room by a crew member. But later he went by himself and was found in a restricted area inside the ship. The crew member reported the incident to Captain Lehmann. But Lehmann doubted that Spah was anything other than what he claimed to be: a professional acrobat and comedian.

In spite of Captain Lehmann's private worries, the two-night trip over the Atlantic was uneventful. In

Captain Max Pruss piloted the *Hindenburg* on its final journey.

the afternoon of the second day, the passengers enjoyed viewing some icebergs that were spotted a few hours before they reached Newfoundland. The sun had finally come out, and Captain Pruss flew low over the icebergs so the passengers could see them up close. There were pools of icy green water in the middle of some of the icebergs, and rainbows circled some of them. Looking down on them, the passengers could see the tips of the icebergs sticking out of the water, and the great bulks looming below the surface. The icebergs reminded Gertrude Adelt of the *Titanic*, the so-called "unsinkable ship" that went down nearby after it hit an iceberg in 1912. Joseph Spah recorded the scene with his home movie camera while Otto Clemens took photographs.

Soon after passing over the icebergs, the *Hindenburg* reached the North American mainland. The green, forested hills of Newfoundland welcomed the travelers. Then Captain Pruss turned the airship south, back out over the ocean toward New York. They would arrive the next day. The passengers enjoyed their last dinner on the *Hindenburg* and relaxed in the lounge before retiring for the night.

and help hold the ship down. The main cables would be immediately shackled to a winch powered by a diesel engine. Dozens of other thin cables, called spider cables, had wooden handles spliced into their ends. The men on the ground would grab these and hold on tight, digging their heels into the dirt, to keep the big airship in place.

Behind Schedule

Rather than pay all these workers to be on the job continually while waiting for the airship to arrive, an arrangement had been worked out to land the *Hindenburg* at either 6 A.M. or 6 P.M. On this trip the *Hindenburg* was scheduled for a 6 A.M. landing. After fighting a strong head wind the entire trip, however, the airship was eight hours behind schedule. The landing was rescheduled for 6 P.M.

Coming down the coast toward Lakehurst, Captain Pruss flew over Boston. He flew the *Hindenburg* low enough so that the passengers could see cars pulling over to the side of the road and people getting out to look up. Passengers who knew the Boston area were able to pick out familiar landmarks below. Large buildings, highways, and bridges looked like tiny models. Gradually, the city gave way to the New England forest. One passenger spotted a group of three deer bounding through the woods. Next, the *Hindenburg* flew over New York City. The *Hindenburg* came in over Long Island Sound on its way into the city. From on board, the view was

Four

The Dream Becomes a Nightmare

May 6 dawned drizzly and dark at Lakehurst, the *Hindenburg*'s final destination. Capt. Charles Rosendahl, supervisor of the ground crew, was keeping a close eye on the weather reports in anticipation of the *Hindenburg*'s arrival. From the Germans' perspective, Rosendahl was the most trusted zeppelin man in the United States. He had piloted the *Los Angeles*, a zeppelin that the Germans had built for the United States and had proven himself to be knowledgeable and capable.

As chief of the ground crew, Rosendahl had assembled more than two hundred men, including more than one hundred from the naval base at Lakehurst. Their duty was to be on hand when the *Hindenburg* arrived, to grab the cables

The *Hindenburg* burns on the ground after exploding on May 6, 1937 in
Lakehurst, New Jersey.

unlike anything the passengers had ever seen. Leonhard Adelt thought the skyscrapers of Manhattan looked like so many nails sticking out of a plank. Adelt was amazed that every detail of New York's hustle and bustle was there, but in ant-sized miniature. The Statue of Liberty looked like a child's delicate porcelain doll, he thought. Above Brooklyn, the *Hindenburg* cruised over Ebbets Field, where the Dodgers were playing the Pittsburgh Pirates. The baseball game was stopped so that fans could take a look at the *Hindenburg* as it cruised overhead.

Dwarfed by Its Immensity

Several airplanes flew alongside the *Hindenburg* and were dwarfed by its immensity. Traffic stopped as drivers craned their necks to look up at the majestic airship, its tail fins proudly displaying Hitler's swastika. Thousands of people saw the *Hindenburg* that day. They followed it across the sky, looking out of windows and from rooftops, fire escapes, and sidewalks. Captain Pruss went over the busy Times Square area before heading for lower Manhattan. He flew over Wall Street, then out over the Hudson River, where tugboats sounded welcoming blasts.

Staying on course for Lakehurst, the *Hindenburg* approached the airfield at 4 P.M. Winds were gusting at up to twenty-eight miles an hour, and dark clouds were threatening to unleash a thunderstorm. The always-cautious Captain Pruss felt that the winds were blowing too strongly

to attempt a landing, so he wrote a note to the ground crew that said "Riding the storm out." He attached it to a weight and dropped it on the field.

Time to Kill

With time to kill, Captain Pruss decided to do some more sight-seeing. Although the passengers had already packed their bags and piled them up near the bust of President von Hindenburg, they did not seem to mind the delay. In fact, they seemed to rather enjoy this unusual method of seeing the sights. Pruss flew the ship over the Toms River, then south along the New Jersey coast to Little Egg Harbor, and out almost to Atlantic City.

While cruising, the *Hindenburg* maintained radio contact with the airfield. At 5:35, the control tower radioed: "Visibility westward eight miles unsettled, recommend delay landing until further word from station." Captain Pruss replied: "We will wait your report that landing conditions are better."

At 6:12, Lakehurst sent this message: "Conditions now considered suitable for landing. Ground crew is ready. . . ." At Captain Pruss's order, Willie Speck radioed back that the ship would land.

At about 7 P.M., Captain Pruss approached the airfield and gradually began decreasing the ship's altitude. On board, the crew followed the routine landing procedures, valving off gas from the dirigible and preparing to drop cables to the ground crew. After a long day of waiting, the ground crew was ready. Families of passengers were also gathered nearby to meet their loved ones. Just outside the main gate, Joseph Spah's wife, Anna, and their three children watched. Margaret Mather's family was also there to pick her up. Two of Leonhard Adelt's brothers waited on the ground. It had been thirty years since he had last seen them.

Also on hand were several newspaper reporters. The *Hindenburg* did not create the sort of stir that the *Graf Zeppelin* had a few years before, but it was still news. A radio announcer was there as well. American Airlines had hired Herb Morrison, an announcer for radio station WLS of Chicago, to report on the *Hindenburg*'s first landing of the season. Through the magic of radio,

Inside the motor gondola of the *Hindenburg*. Could a bomb, planted deep within the recesses of the *Hindenburg*, have caused it to explode?

Morrison would provide listeners with a mental picture of the majestic airship as it delivered its first passengers of the season.

"A Marvelous Sight"

All eyes were on the *Hindenburg* as Captain Pruss made the final maneuvers to swing the nose of the craft into place at the mooring mast. By 7:19 the *Hindenburg* had come to a complete stop. It was about two hundred feet up, floating next to the mooring mast. The spring evening was just turning dark. Announcer Herb Morrison relayed the sight to his listeners: "Here it comes, ladies and gentlemen, and what a sight it is, a thrilling one, a marvelous sight. . . . The sun is striking the windows of the observation deck on the western side and sparkling like glittering jewels on the background of black velvet."

The stern, or rear, of the ship was slightly lower than the bow, or front part. This was because the rainwater that had soaked the *Hindenburg*'s fabric skin during the day rolled to the back of the airship as it moved forward through the air. Captain Pruss compensated by ordering six crewmen to the nose of the ship. Their combined weight would level the ship.

The forward and aft engines were idling, in case the captain needed a quick thrust in any direction. A sudden gust of wind came up, pushing the *Hindenburg* to starboard, the right side. Captain Pruss made a quick turn to keep the nose of the airship in position next to the

The giant *Hindenburg* crashes to earth after bursting into flames.

mooring mast. At 7:21 the main cables in the front and back of the ship were dropped to the ground. The men below picked up the cables and prepared to shackle them to the winch.

Inside the ship, crewmen were at their landing stations, preparing to drop the several dozen remaining spider cables. In the tail section near the rear of the ship, Hans Fruend and Helmut Lau were working to untangle a cable that had become stuck. Lau was at the top of a thirty-foot stairway, and Fruend was at the bottom. It was 7:23.

Looking up at Lau for a moment, Fruend noticed a small blue and white flash inside one of the gas bags above and behind Lau. He also heard a muffled pop. Lau heard it, too. He turned around to watch as the flash quickly grew into a flickering yellow and orange flame. Both men watched the small blaze take hold. Then the gas bag suddenly disintegrated from the heat as a red-orange fireball raced upward. In the next instant a huge explosion rocked the ship. A tremendous ball of brilliant fire and black smoke mushroomed out through the top of the *Hindenburg*. Fueled by seven million cubic feet of hydrogen, the explosion consumed the rear part of the ship instantly. The *Hindenburg* went crashing down into the mooring mast as the flames raced

The death of the *Hindenburg*. The extreme flammability of the hydrogen gas inside the *Hindenburg* caused its quick end. In just thirty-four seconds, a small spark developed into a huge, all-consuming fire. These pictures reveal the *Hindenburg's* total destruction.

People are seen running from the burning wreckage of the *Hindenburg*.
Remarkably, many passengers survived the explosion.

toward the bow.

The dreamy picture that Morrison had created for his listeners suddenly became a nightmare: "Oh, oh, oh! . . . It burst into flame! It burst into flame and it's falling . . . ladies and gentlemen this is terrible! This is one of the worst catastrophes in the world, all the humanity . . . ladies and gentlemen you'll have to excuse me, I can't talk . . . this is the worst thing I've ever witnessed."

On the A and B decks in the ship's hull, some of the passengers and crew members were knocked to the floor by the explosion. They struggled to their feet as the entire ship tilted toward the stern. In the confusion, they did not immediately realize what had happened. Looking out of the windows, they saw the men of the ground crew first freeze in terror, then turn and run. An eerie pink glow reflected off the ground below, as if of a brilliant sunset. The fire started off the bow and traveled toward the stern. The passengers understood that the *Hindenburg* was burning above them.

Fortunately for Fruend and Lau, the flames went upward as the stern came crashing down. When it hit the ground, they climbed out. Meanwhile, the bow of the airship went higher into the air. Its fabric skin was peeling off in burning sheets. Pieces of burning fabric and white-hot metal rained down on the airfield. As the bow continued rising into the air, eleven of the twelve crew members in the nose section fell sliding into the flames, while one, Joseph Liebrandt, hung on for his life. Finally, the bow was pointing straight up. Then, like a giant blow torch, one huge long flame shot out through the nose of the ship and up into the sky.

Joseph Spah was at one of the windows in the dining room when the explosion occurred. Otto Clemens was taking pictures, and Spah was filming the landing with his movie camera. After the explosion, Spah's first instinct was to jump. He used his camera to break the window. The camera case slipped off his shoulder, and he watched it fall to the ground. It seemed like a long way down. The bow section was rising still higher.

Spah and two other men held onto the window ledge. One of the men jumped feet-first while they were still more than one hundred feet from the ground. Spah watched the man hit the dirt with a sickening thud. He decided to hang on for a bit. Spah waited until the ground was about forty feet away, then put his acrobatic training to use. Hanging by his arms out of the window, he let go of the ledge, remembering to keep his knees bent. He landed on his feet and then

The blackened remains of the *Hindenburg's* twisted skeleton.

rolled. He stood up and walked away with a limp.

Others on board were not sure what to do. One woman dropped her two children out of a window from about fifteen feet, one at a time. Some men below caught them both and carried them away from the fire. Other people on board held on to whatever they could. Some plunged to the earth, flailing their arms and legs as they fell. Long flames shot down the hallways of the *Hindenburg*.

Some of the passengers waited until they felt the airship hit the ground and then ran for their lives through the scorching flames. One man sat on the steps between decks and waited until he felt the crash of the ship hitting the ground. Then he jumped through a nearby window frame. He landed on his hands and knees, then got up and ran.

Certain Death

Gertrude and Leonhard Adelt jumped, but they could not remember when. Leonhard used his bare hands to pry apart pieces of the white-hot metal frame of the airship. He felt no pain, however. It was all very dreamlike. He remembered letting go of his wife's hand and jumping out of the ship, then turning back to see his wife lying still on the ground. He went back to her, pulled her up, and gave her a push. She began running, but he fell to the ground. He felt strangely peaceful and thought of staying there, even though he knew it meant certain death. But then he lifted his head and saw Gertrude again, running through the smoke. He got up and went to her. Looking back at the burning wreck, he felt strangely attracted to the flames. He wanted to go back to the airship, but she prevented him.

The *Hindenburg* Had Landed

Like Joseph Spah, Margaret Mather was also in the dining room when the explosion occurred. But she did not jump. She was thrown against one wall, with a pile of men on top of her. She was afraid she would suffocate there. But after the men jumped up, she remained sitting, watching as the airship was tossed to and fro on its final descent. People were crashing into railings and furniture. They were bleeding. She saw long yellow and red flames shooting through the room. She watched as several people jumped out of the windows. Some screamed as they went. It reminded her of Dante's *Inferno*. She covered her face with her coat and patted out the occasional flames in her hair and on her coat. She stayed huddled against the wall for what seemed a long time. Finally, she heard someone yell, "Come out, lady!" The *Hindenburg* had landed. She hopped out through its burning remains.

Werner Franz, a cabin boy, was near the officers' mess when the airship blew up. He looked for the gangway as the ship pitched back and forth, but he could not find it. He could not find anything, because he was surrounded by fire.

Then one of the bags that contained water ballast burst over his head. It doused him with about two tons of water and probably saved his life. He found an escape hatch near the smoking room and jumped through it.

The men in the command gondola were among the last to know what had happened. Captain Lehmann was there. He asked Captain Pruss if one of the cables had broken. "No," said Pruss. "What is it?"

A crewman picked up the phone to call the tail section, but the line was dead. Finally, they heard radio chief Willie Speck shout that the ship was on fire. Captain Pruss made the quick decision not to dump the water ballast in the bow of the ship. He hoped that the weight of the water would bring the ship down to earth and allow at least those in the bow to survive.

"Stand Fast!"

On the ground, people were running away from the *Hindenburg* as fast as they could. Burning debris littered the ground, and thick smoke filled the air. There was a roar of flames. Shouts and screams added to the chaos. But when Chief Boatswain "Bull" Tobin bellowed, "Stand fast!" the men of the ground crew turned back toward the downed airship. They began jumping into the flames and pulling out injured people and the bodies of those who did not survive.

The fire burned the ropes that held the gangway, and it dropped down to the ground. Mr. and Mrs. Ernst walked arm in arm down the gangway stairs almost as if it were a normal landing. Two men grabbed their arms and helped them away from the ship.

"An Infernal Machine"

Edward Douglas, the advertising executive, did not make it out of the flames. Captain Pruss did, with bad burns. Captain Lehmann apparently thought a bomb had caused the explosion. He came stumbling out of the smoldering wreckage muttering, "It must have been an infernal machine." From his neck to his tailbone, his entire back was badly burned.

After the roar of flames died down, the sound of sirens filled the air. Fire trucks and ambulances arrived, and the survivors were carted off to the nearby naval hospital and other hospitals in the area. One of the hangars at the airfield was set up as a temporary morgue.

Thirty-seven years after Count von Zeppelin had launched his dream at Lake Constance, the *Hindenburg* was destroyed in thirty-four seconds at Lakehurst. All that was left of the *Hindenburg* was a blackened, twisted metal skeleton sitting in the dirt. Thirteen passengers, twenty-two crew members, and one member of the ground crew were dead. Sixty-two of the passengers and crew survived.

Five

The Investigation: Why Did the *Hindenburg* Explode?

Less than one hour after the once-mighty *Hindenburg* crumpled to the ground at Lakehurst, Hugo Eckener's phone rang in Germany. It was 2 A.M. The caller was the Berlin correspondent of *The New York Times*. He had bad news for the world's foremost airship expert and the man behind the *Hindenburg*. Upon hearing of the disaster, Eckener immediately began making plans to travel by boat to Lakehurst. He would travel with his chief engineer, Ludwig Durr, and other German technical experts. When they reached the scene eight days later, Eckener surveyed the charred wreckage and murmured, *"Trau-rig,"* the German word meaning

"sad." Then he wept.

Passengers on board the other great German airship, the *Graf Zeppelin,* did not hear the news right away. They were returning to Germany from Rio de Janeiro. The ship's radio operator received a message that the *Hindenburg* had crashed and burned. The report was so unexpected that the captain of the *Graf Zeppelin* assumed it was a hoax. He refused to believe it until he received another message from Germany confirming the disaster. Then he decided that rather than upset the passengers of the *Graf Zeppelin,* he would not tell them the news until the ship landed. These passengers were the last people to ever travel on a commercial passenger zeppelin.

The loss of the *Hindenburg* and all it meant to Germany was devastating. Germany had not only lost its greatest airship but also some of its most prominent citizens. Captain Lehmann, fifty-one, one of Germany's most talented and dedicated airshipmen, died of his wounds the day after the disaster. The casualties also included chief rigger Ludwig Knorr and chief radio operator Willie Speck.

Airship Was Considered Safe

In Germany, the United States, and around the world, one question was in everyone's mind in the days following the disaster: What caused the *Hindenburg* to explode? The disaster was totally unexpected. The airship was considered very safe, despite the knowledge of the extreme

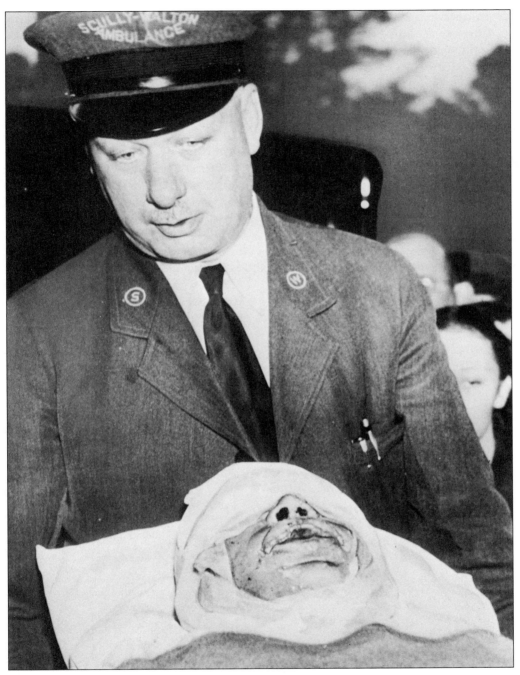

Captain Max Pruss is carried to an ambulance after the *Hindenburg* explosion. Pruss was one of the people who believed the explosion had been deliberately caused by sabotage.

flammability of hydrogen.

Obviously, something had gone terribly wrong. But despite the official U.S. and German investigations that began immediately after the disaster, it remains a mystery.

In the United States, the Department of Commerce appointed a board of inquiry, which began investigating immediately. The board interviewed more than 150 eyewitnesses and listened to the testimony of scientific experts in aviation and molecular physics.

There were many false leads. Some of the witnesses said that sparks from one of the engines caused the accident, even though the explosion took place far from the engines. One scientist believed the disaster was caused by a mysterious "demon proton" in hydrogen that somehow triggered the explosion. Another scientist believed that a loose propeller spun off one of the engine cars and tore into the ship. If it tore into one of the gas bags, it would have allowed some of the hydrogen to escape and could have created an igniting spark by hitting metal. But surely someone would have seen this happen.

There were unproven sabotage theories as well. Some speculated that a bullet was purposely fired into the *Hindenburg*, triggering the explosion. Again, no one could corroborate the story. Both Captain Pruss and Captain Rosendahl said they thought it was a case of sabotage, even though there was no conclusive evidence.

The ominous letter that caused so much suspicion among the Germans before the trip began also turned out to be a fruitless lead.

Survivors escape the burning wreckage.

Kathie Rauch of Milwaukee had simply passed along the vision of a psychic, who said that he dreamed of seeing the *Hindenburg* on fire.

The passengers under suspicion turned out to be innocent as well. The messages received by advertising executive Edward Douglas had been sent in code as a precaution, just in case the information fell into the hands of a competitor in the advertising business. Joseph Spah was also proven to be innocent of wrongdoing.

After dismissing many questionable theories, the board of inquiry decided that there were several possible reasons for the disaster. The most plausible explanations included structural failure, Saint Elmo's fire, static electricity, and sabotage. Each of these explana-tions required a combination of several unlikely events. To the board, none seemed any more likely than the others. The members of the board concluded "No completely certain proof has been found for any of the possibilities cited."

Although the board failed to present a definite finding, it did provide background information on the possibilities. In the case of structural failure, investigators theorized that a cable inside the ship could have snapped as the *Hindenburg* was preparing to dock. This could have happened at the moment when the sudden gust of wind came up and Captain Pruss made a sharp turn to keep the nose of the *Hindenburg* next to the mooring mast. The sharp turn may have increased the tension in an already taut cable,

53

causing it to snap. As it whipped loose, the cable could have slashed through one of the hydrogen-filled bags inside the ship. Hydrogen would have been released and could have been ignited by a spark when the cable came into contact with another piece of metal inside the ship. No one actually saw anything like this happen. Nonetheless, Hugo Eckener was among those who believed in this theory.

Saint Elmo's fire, previously considered a harmless phenomenon, also could have caused the disaster, according to the U.S. board of inquiry. The peculiar phenomenon of built-up crackling static electricity could have ignited some hydrogen that had escaped from the bags. Small amounts of hydrogen were routinely released before landing. The investigators speculated that at Lakehurst, perhaps one of the valves became stuck and continued to release hydrogen. This free hydrogen was then ignited by Saint Elmo's fire. Again, there was no evidence at the time to suggest that this actually happened. But years later, two reliable witnesses testified that they saw Saint Elmo's fire on the top ridge of the airship shortly before the explosion took place.

A Third Possibility

The third possibility cited by the board was static electricity. It could have been present due to the thunderstorm that had recently passed through the area. This explanation was similar to the Saint Elmo's fire theory. The difference would be the presence of a conductor that would touch off a spark. Investigators thought that either the ship's water ballast or the cables that were dropped to the ground could have served as a conductor, creating the spark necessary to ignite some free-floating hydrogen.

Finally, there was the possibility of sabotage. There was nothing to document the idea that anyone purposely had acted to destroy or damage the *Hindenburg*. There were not even any well-formed sabotage theories. Yet the board did not rule out the possibility.

Failed to Find Definite Cause

The German commission was nearly as inconclusive as the U.S. inquiry. It also failed to find any definite cause but would not dismiss the possibility of sabotage. Part of the German commission's report said: "The possibility of deliberate destruction must be admitted, since no other originating cause can be proven."

It was the Third Reich's policy, however, to never admit to any weakness. The idea of saboteurs bringing down the mighty *Hindenburg* was not acceptable to the German government, nor was the idea that a flaw in the design of the ship, or even simple human error, could have been responsible. Therefore, Hitler declared the disaster an act of God.

While Hitler would have liked to close the book on the *Hindenburg* forever, people still have not forgotten it. The disaster was so spectacular that it continued to fascinate

Was the *Hindenburg* destroyed by someone who hated the Nazi regime?
Author Michael Mooney McDonald believes so.

people years later. With no clear official explanation ever offered, many still think it was an act of sabotage.

In 1972, thirty-five years after the disaster, a book published by Michael Mooney McDonald presented new evidence on how an act of sabotage could have taken place within the established facts of the case. McDonald described how a crew member could have planted an explosive device in the lining of one of the *Hindenburg*'s gas cells.

McDonald believes that the crew member was Eric Spehl, who did not agree with Hitler's policies. Spehl's motive for destroying the *Hindenburg* would have been to demonstrate his opposition to the Third Reich. According to McDonald, Spehl may have made a simple bomb with a battery and a flash-bulb and slipped it into a fold in one of the gas bags during the trip to Lakehurst. He would then have set the timer on his bomb, assuming that the *Hindenburg* would make its 6 P.M. landing on schedule. The airship would then have been empty when the explosion took place around 7:20 P.M., and no one would have been injured. Because of the bad weather, however, the landing was delayed, and the bomb went off when the ship was still in the air and full of passengers.

Accounts of the way the fire started seem to support McDonald's theory. While burning hydrogen creates a characteristic white light, the first flames that people saw were yellow. This and the initial small explosion witnessed by crewmen Helmut Lau and Hans Fruend

55

AN ENDURING SAGA

More than half a century after the disaster, the *Hindenburg* continues to intrigue people. Some of the interest is due to the film footage and radio recordings of the event, which have allowed people to see and hear about the disaster decades after it happened.

Until the 1930s, news was communicated primarily through written accounts and radio reports. When disasters occurred, like the sinking of the *Titanic* in 1912, people learned about them in the newspapers. Through reading eyewitness accounts, people did their best to imagine what had happened. If someone with a camera happened to be on the scene, a newspaper story might be illustrated with photographs.

But as the technology for moving pictures improved, people began filming newsworthy events. Television was not yet available, but the film was distributed to movie theaters across the country. When people went to see a movie, they first saw filmed coverage of current events.

The disaster at Lakehurst was captured on film, and millions of people experienced the *Hindenburg's* inferno within days of the tragedy. It was as if they had been there watching. They saw the horrifying explosion, the flames engulfing the airship, and the people jumping out as it fell to the ground. In effect, people all around the world witnessed the disaster. The emotional impact on viewers was powerful and immediate.

would be typical events that occur with the type of bomb McDonald said Spehl planted.

Other than this kind of circumstantial evidence, however, there is little to substantiate McDonald's story. The day after the *Hindenburg* exploded, Spehl died of the injuries he received in the disaster. Any physical evidence of a bomb would also have perished in the disaster. McDonald makes the case that Spehl acted alone but that his girlfriend in Germany may have known about his plan. No one there has ever come forth with any definite evidence of such a bombing, however.

Whatever the cause of the disaster, May 6, 1937, marked the passing of an era. To airship pioneer Hugo Eckener, the burned-out skeleton at Lakehurst symbolized the result of his life's work. He wrote: "It appeared to me the hopeless end of a great dream, a kind of end of the world."

Shortsighted Overconfidence

In the days following the disaster, the Germans insisted that they would continue using hydrogen-filled airships. But before long, they grounded the *Graf Zeppelin* forever. Once proud signs of superior German engineering and know-how, the gigantic zeppelins became symbols of shortsighted overconfidence.

The precise engineering of Ludwig Durr and the careful attention of pilots like Hugo Eckener had been enough to allow the *Graf Zeppelin* to operate for ten years without an accident. The Zeppelin Corporation had hoped to continue that remarkable record of safety with the *Hindenburg*. But no matter how cautious and meticulous the Germans were, they could not make their airships disaster-proof.

The Limits of Technology

The *Hindenburg*'s demise illustrates once again the limits of technology. Just as the double-hulled *Titanic* had been thought by some to be unsinkable, the *Hindenburg* was assumed to be absolutely safe. Both incidents taught the hard lesson that the use of technology inevitably involves risk. Ingenious human devices like dirigibles can allow people to achieve the impossible. But there is never a guarantee that human handiwork—no matter how well engineered—is absolutely safe.

Two years after the disaster at Lakehurst, another proud German dream of invincibility was finally launched. On September 1, 1939, Hitler's troops invaded Poland. France and Britain immediately declared war on Germany. Over the next six years, the universal catastrophe of World War II played itself out in countless acts of fiery destruction. World War II dwarfed the disaster of the *Hindenburg*, sensational though it was.

Epilogue
An Almost-Forgotten Legacy

The destruction of the *Hindenburg* is reminiscent of other technological feats gone wrong, such as the sinking of the *Titanic* in 1912 or the explosion of the space shuttle *Challenger* in 1986. Like these other disasters, the event was so spectacular that it commanded the attention of the world and will never be forgotten.

The widespread news footage of the *Hindenburg* explosion was played again and again in movie theaters around the world. Simultaneously, the huge airships lost their reputation for safety and unrivaled luxury. The use of zeppelins for travel ended as abruptly as the explosion at Lakehurst. People did not miss the lesson played out on the screen: the highly flammable hydrogen gas was simply too dangerous to use. The huge airships became a thing of the past, and airplanes quickly replaced them.

The *Hindenburg* and other dirigibles, however, were becoming obsolete before the disaster. As happens with technological breakthroughs, each successive invention quickly replaces what went before it. In this way, automobiles quickly replaced the horse and buggy, and electricity caused people to abandon their oil lamps. And sometimes, on the road of progress, an invention fails and human lives are lost in the process. Certainly, one of the lessons of progress is to learn from the past how to make sure safety keeps pace with the need for faster, improved machinery.

In the rush to get airborne people believed that dirigibles, even though they were filled with dangerous gas, were a quick and efficient method of air travel. After the *Hindenburg* explosion, such a risk did not seem worthwhile when the alternative was an even faster, even more efficient machine—the airplane.

Blimps

While never again filled with hydrogen, and never again used for passenger travel, dirigibles containing nonflammable helium gas have occasionally been flown. The U.S. Navy used helium-filled dirigibles for antisubmarine patrols in World War II and continued to experiment with them throughout the 1950s. These dirigibles were much smaller and did not require a rigid internal frame like the zeppelins. These nonrigid, helium-filled dirigibles are more commonly known as blimps.

In March 1957, the U.S. Navy blimp *Snowbird* flew from South Weymouth, Massachusetts, to Europe and returned to Key West, Florida, without refueling. The eleven-day flight demonstrated the dirigible's unique ability to soar with little fuel. Nonetheless, the dirigible's main drawback—the lack of speed—was still there, and the Navy stopped building blimps in 1962. In an age when planes could break the sound barrier by achieving incredible speeds, the dirigible seemed like an almost worthless invention.

Some of the few successful modern dirigibles since the *Hindenburg* have been the well-known blimps of the Goodyear Tire and Rubber Company. Goodyear signed a contract with the Germans in the late 1920s to use the Zeppelin Corporation's patents on helium-filled airships in the United States. Over the years, Goodyear has built more than three hundred blimps, including many for the Navy. Much smaller than the German zeppelins, Goodyear's standard blimps measure 192 feet long and 50 feet in diameter, with a volume of 202,000 cubic feet.

Today, Goodyear operates a fleet of four blimps: the *Enterprise,* based in Pompano Beach, Florida; the *America,* based in Houston, Texas; the *Columbia,* based in Los Angeles, California; and the *Europa,* based near Rome, Italy. All but the *Europa* are named after yachts that have won the America's Cup trophy.

The Goodyear blimp's familiar shape is often seen over major outdoor events like the Super Bowl, the World Series, and the Indianapolis 500. These well-publicized events have increased popular recognition of the Goodyear blimps, as the blimps have in turn publicized the Goodyear Company. While the blimps perform no function other than a public relations one, they do this extremely well. Nearly everyone has heard of the Goodyear blimp.

Blimps Continue to Be Useful

In a limited capacity, other dirigibles have been used by scientists. The National Aeronautics and Space Administration (NASA) has stationed experimental helium-filled balloons high in the earth's atmosphere. In 1988 and again in 1990, NASA launched a two-ton probe that was held aloft by a helium-filled balloon. Taking advantage of the unique capabilities of dirigible flight, the probe was used to measure radiation from distant stars. In this way, the dirigible continues to be useful in scientific pursuits.

But for the most part, dreams of practical uses for the dirigible died on the fateful evening the *Hindenburg* exploded. But the larger dream, to build inventions that can carry more people farther than before, remains. As the United States and other countries tentatively plan a trip to Mars, the search for new frontiers will forever be one of humanity's strongest urges.

Glossary

aft: Toward the rear of a ship or aircraft.

airship: An aircraft that is lighter than air and has mechanisms for steering and propulsion. A rigid airship, or zeppelin, has an internal metal frame that holds bags of gas. A non-rigid airship, or blimp, has no frame, and maintains its shape due to the pressure of the gas inside it.

ballast: Weight that is carried, usually in the form of water, to improve the stability and control the ascent of an airship.

blimp: A non-rigid airship. Supposedly the name originated in World War I when Lt. A.D. Cunningham of Great Britain's Royal Navy Air Service was conducting his weekly inspection of a British airship. Cunningham flipped his thumb at the envelope of the aircraft, and a strange noise echoed off the tight fabric cover. Imitating the sound, Cunningham cried out, "Blimp!"

bow: The front of the ship.

DELAG: The German Airship Transport Company, (in German, Deutsche Luftschiffharts Aktein Gellschaft) the first airline in the world, started by Count Ferdinand von Zeppelin in 1909.

dirigible: An airship, either rigid or non-rigid.

elevator: A movable surface on the tail fin of an airship. Flipping the elevators up or down steers the craft.

envelope: The bag containing the gas in an airship.

helium: A non-flammable lighter-than-air gas, used to inflate airships.

hydrogen: a flammable lighter-than-air gas, discovered by Henry Cavendish in 1766, used to supply the lift in airships like the *Hindenburg*.

keel: The wooden assembly attached to the bottom of an airship.

Nazism: Political and economic doctrines put into effect by the National Socialist German Workers' Party from 1933 to 1945 under Adolf Hitler and his followers.

propaganda: The spreading of ideas, information or rumors for the purpose of helping or hurting an institution or country.

sabotage: The deliberate destruction of property designed to hinder a nation's war effort.

Saint Elmo's Fire: A flaming phenomenon sometimes seen in stormy weather on aircraft and ships, caused by the discharge of static electricity.

stern: The rear of an aircraft or ship.

swastika: Symbol of Nazism; a Greek cross with the ends of the arms extended at right angles in the same direction.

transatlantic: Crossing or extending across the Atlantic Ocean.

zeppelin: A rigid airship built by Germans.

Suggestions for Further Reading

Botting, Douglas, *The Giant Airships.* New York: Dodd, Mead and Company, 1972.

Compton's Encyclopedia. Chicago: Encyclopaedia Britannica, Inc., 1989 Edition.

Larson, George, *Blimp!* New York: Van Nostrand Reinhold Company, 1981.

Larson, George, *The Blimp Book.* Mill Valley, CA; Squarebooks, 1977.

Mooney, Michael M., *The Hindenburg.* New York: Dodd, Mead and Company, 1972.

Woods, Peter, *When Zeppelins Flew.* New York: Time-Life Books, 1969.

Works Consulted

Dick, Harold G., with Robinson, Douglas H., *The Golden Age of the Great Passenger Airships: Graf Zeppelin and Hindenburg.* Washington, DC: Smithsonian Institution Press, 1985.

Horton, Edward, *The Age of the Airship.* Chicago: Henry Regnery Co., 1973.

Jackson, Robert, *Airships: A Popular History of Dirigibles, Zeppelins, Blimps and Other Lighter-Than-Air Craft.* Garden City, NY: Doubleday and Company, 1973.

McPhee, John, *The Deltoid Pumpkin Seed.* New York: Farrar, Straus and Giroux, 1973.

Robinson, Douglas H., *Famous Aircraft: The LZ 129 "Hindenburg."* New York: Arco Publishing Company, 1964.

Robinson, Douglas H., *Giants in the Sky.* Seattle, WA: University of Washington Press, 1973.

Shirer, William L., *The Rise and Fall of the Third Reich: A History of Nazi Germany.* New York: Simon and Schuster, 1960.

Welch, David, ed. *Nazi Propaganda.* Beckenham, Kent: Croom Helm Ltd., 1983.

Index

About the Author and Illustrator

The Author, Tom Stacey, is a graduate of Michigan State University. He has worked as a reporter and editor for several West Coast newspapers, and now lives and works as a freelance writer in La Jolla, California.

The Illustrator, Brian McGovern, has been active in both fine art and commercial illustration for twenty years. His recent clients include AT&T, DuPont, Harvey's Lake Tahoe, and Chase Manhattan Bank. He has exhibited paintings in San Francisco and New York and was recently a published winner in *American Artists Magazine* in the "Preserving Our National Wilderness" competition. He has won several Best of Show awards in the fantasy art field and the 1987 Distinguished Leadership Award from American Biographical Institute in North Carolina.

Picture Credits

DATE DUE		
MY7 '99		
JA 18 '00		
MR 10 '00		
MR 29 '00		
AP 4 '00		
AP 12 '00		

98-481

363.12   Stacey, Thomas,
STA   The Hindenburg